A Space for Faith

A Space for Faith

The Colonial Meetinghouses of New England

Paul Wainwright, Photographer

Essay by Peter Benes
Foreword by Brent D. Glass
Commentary by William E. Williams

Published by Jetty House
An imprint of Peter E. Randall Publisher
Portsmouth, NH

Published by Jetty House
An imprint of Peter E. Randall Publisher
Box 4726, Portsmouth, NH 03802-4726
www.perpublisher.com

(ISBN 13) 978-0-9817898-5-9
(ISBN 10) 0-981-7898-5-4

Library of Congress Control Number: 2009939458

Publication of this book has been supported by grants from:

Quotations from hymns by William Billings (1746–1800) were obtained from the Choral Public Domain Library (www.cpdl.org), and are used in accord with the CPDL License which ensures the freedom to distribute and perform music that is in the public domain.

Additional copies of this book can be purchased by visiting:
www.aspaceforfaith.com

Printed in China

Book design and composition by Ed Stevens
www.edstevensdesign.com

To Judy: persistent advocate, honest critic, best friend

Contents

Foreword

"We're taking a vote." That cell phone message from one of the passengers on United Flight 93 preceded the dramatic rebellion on the hijacked airplane that crashed moments later in a Pennsylvania field on September 11, 2001. In less than thirty minutes, these heroic citizens had organized themselves, developed a plan, and then taken a vote and acted collectively to save their lives and the lives of potentially thousands of people on the ground.

At that moment of extreme urgency and crisis, a form of town meeting took place on Flight 93, a brief but poignant tribute to traditions that are deeply embedded in Americans from a variety of backgrounds. The setting aboard that plane was vastly different from the meetinghouses pictured in this book. Nevertheless, Flight 93 became a meetinghouse in the sky, and its story illustrates that the ideals that flourished in these simple buildings of faith and community have endured over the centuries and have shaped our national character.

In his remarkable study of early American folkways, *Albion's Seed* (1989), historian David Hackett Fischer traces the origins of meetinghouses and town meetings to the rural settlements of East Anglia in England. He also notes that the town meetings in New England were "not really democratic.... The object was not rule by majority, but by consensus." Through "discussion, persuasion, and mutual adjustment of differences," participants reached an understanding of "the will of the town."

The Mayflower Compact, written and signed even before the Pilgrims landed in Plymouth, reflected the political philosophy that prevailed in New England. In creating their government and the procedure for making "just and equal laws," they were codifying more than an administrative procedure. Their larger objective was to foster a sense of community, a spirit of civic life in a strange and new world. The meetinghouse was the place where they practiced and refined this experiment in self-government in what John Winthrop called "a city on the hill."

This concept of making decisions through mutual self-interest is at the heart of American democracy. In *The Federalist* (1788), for example, James Madison wrote that, in a large representative democracy like the United States, the competing claims of various factions would come under control through the necessity to compromise and negotiate differences and conflicts. Alexis de Tocqueville, in *Democracy in America* (1835-40), commented on the powerful and favorable influence of New England townships in fostering a spirit of independence and local authority, hallmarks of a democratic society.

The physical survival of meetinghouses is remarkable given the pace of change in our country over the past four centuries. They provide a tangible anchor on the town square, landmarks of the social compact. Although we have often fallen short of that ideal of civic virtue and mutuality, the meetinghouse is there to remind us and challenge us. To understand the significance of the New England meetinghouse is to understand the power and the promise of the American Dream.

Brent D. Glass

Washington, D.C.
November 2008

Brent Glass is the Elizabeth MacMillan Director of the National Museum of American History at the Smithsonian Institution and a member of the Flight 93 Memorial Commission.

Commentary

Interiors as Beacons of Light

Paul Wainwright's photographs of New England meetinghouses are about physical space; simultaneously they serve as locators of American identity and culture. Wainwright uses a four-by-five-inch view camera to draw and compose on the ground glass. It is the only camera type capable of capturing both the physical and ethereal qualities of these buildings. Constructed from virginal forests, they are New World adaptations of Old World building types. The activities they housed, from town meetings to Sunday worship services, represent the earliest manifestations of American civic and religious life—which had roots in the Old World but evolved into something new and vital.

These buildings, scattered throughout the region, incorporate the finest carpentry, ironwork, and plain old Yankee ingenuity into their being. Wainwright has made them palpable in his chosen medium of photography. His working methods are traditional; he uses film to make negatives and light-sensitive paper to make prints from the negatives. Wainwright's exactitude in his use of the camera and these materials situate his work between documentation and interpretive photography.

His photographs share subject matter and themes with Charles Sheeler, Paul Strand, Walker Evans, Paul Caponigro, and Linda Connor in the twentieth century. All of these photographers, beginning with Sheeler and Strand, have photographed American vernacular architecture and space with documentary clarity while producing interpretive works of photographic art. Walker Evans, in a 1971 interview in *Art in America Magazine*, defined this way of working as "documentary style"—harnessing objectivity to subjective intuition. This approach has its origins in American photography beginning with the nineteenth-century view-camera photographs of George Barnard's Civil War battlefields, Timothy O'Sullivan's images of the American Western landscape, Carleton Watkins' majestic mammoth-plate (seventeen-by-twenty-inch) depictions of Yosemite, and Josiah Johnson Hawes' urban views of Boston. Their work became visual documents that define American culture and identity.

Paul Strand has made some of the most memorable photographs of New England meetinghouses. They appeared in *Time in New England*, published in 1950 alongside text edited by Nancy Newhall to evoke the region's visual and literary culture. Charles Sheeler's photographs of Chartres Cathedral, made some thirty years earlier, were photographed in series to yield a more comprehensive presentation than could be made by any one photograph. Wainwright's intimate images, made in various locales, form a composite representation of the New England Meetinghouse. The photographer's fidelity to the representation of light as form unifies the series. It also provides the means through which the ineffable is invoked. In their photographs of sacred sites, Linda Connor and Paul Caponigro use light in a similar way to connote the spiritual and sacred.

Evans and Strand are known for photographing architectural exteriors as a continuous aspect of the man-made landscape. Strand's New England meetinghouse pictures in *Time in New England*, beginning with the one printed on the cover, function as a composite portrait of the exterior of these buildings, just as Sheeler's photographs of Chartres do. Wainwright, unlike Strand and Sheeler, has chosen to make a composite portrait of the *interiors* of these buildings, emphasizing their communal and individual use. Through his exterior images, he invites the viewer to experience the austere interiors, defined by centuries-old patinas. Natural light, filtered through ancient handmade-glass windows, spotlights and highlights these spaces. The light is so precisely evoked that it is difficult to believe its only source is the sun. Some of Wainwright's exposures lasted up to thirty-five minutes, with the view-camera lens set at a small aperture for maximum sharpness from near to far. This technique renders space and surfaces with sculptural verisimilitude. The composite interior spaces and the details therein of benches, stairs, windows, and roof trusses become representative of the past as the viewer experiences the present. Paul Wainwright's intelligent and passionate photographs of American material culture are superb art and a fitting testament to the builders and users of these meetinghouses.

William Earle Williams

Haverford, Pennsylvania
January 2009

William Williams is the Audrey A. and John L. Dusseau Professor in the Humanities and Curator of Photography at Haverford College in Haverford, Pennsylvania.

Preface

My passion for photographing old buildings reflects my curiosity about exploring the experience of living by examining the structures we build, which, without our realizing it, become monuments to our way of life.

New England's colonial meetinghouses were built to serve the needs of a community to gather both for town business and religious worship—concepts that were not at all distinct in colonial New England before the separation of church and state. While many of these meetinghouses have been torn down or renovated well beyond their original appearance, the structures included in this book and accompanying exhibition look much as they did when they were first built. I feel a "presence" whenever I am in one of these places—not in a haunting way, but with a sense of wonderment about the people who built and used them. My photographs of these structures are devoid of people, yet to me they are all about our nation's ancestors, whose lives—the day-to-day joys and cares—are not much different from mine today. Sometimes when I am in one of these meetinghouses I love to sit and contemplate those who came

before me. I wonder how many others have had the same experience.

In photographing these buildings, I have made every effort to omit any reference to the nineteenth, twentieth, or twenty-first centuries. For example, my preferred interpretation of exterior views is straight on and square. Telephone wires frequently require that I relax this approach. Also, when photographing the interior spaces, I always use natural light. I feel that artificial illumination would detract from the sense of space and light that I experience in these places. Furthermore, most of these meetinghouses to this day do not have electricity.

While architectural photographs are usually seen as illustrations of what a structure looks like, this is not my primary intent. Rather, I see beauty and mystery in these meetinghouses. I love the textures of the wood. I am impressed with their regularity and symmetry—they are beautiful in their austerity and simplicity. Perhaps romantically, I suspect these qualities reflect the lives of those who built them. Their religious beliefs were unambiguous and the simple lines of their meetinghouses reflect this.

In many ways, the location where each photograph was made is unimportant. I approach meetinghouses in much the same way that an artist who works with the human form approaches a model. It is not important what the person's name is. Rather, the artist sees in the model a quality that can, when properly posed and lit, yield a piece of art. These meetinghouses are my "models" for making art, and my photographs reflect my emotional response to them—my physical location when I made each photograph is not of primary importance. Therefore, the images in this book are sequenced for artistic purposes, and not by where they were made.

I made my first photograph of a meetinghouse in Fremont, New Hampshire, a town not far from where I live. That led to several nearby meetinghouses in Sandown and Danville, New Hampshire. Following my curiosity, I started to do some reading to find additional structures that would pose for me as models. I began to understand the importance of the history embodied in these places, and the project began to take shape.

My photographs are first seen in my mind before they are made. My craft with working the camera, developing the negative, and making the print is then harnessed to produce the desired image. The slow pace of working with a traditional wooden field camera, sheet film, chemicals, and photographic paper causes me—*forces* me—to slow down and think. I enjoy the tactile quality of working with traditional photographic media. There is an intimacy in going under the dark cloth and looking at an upside-down image on the ground glass or in working in the darkroom on a snowy winter day. I hope that this feeling is reflected in my photographs. There is certainly a Zen-like quality to my pace of working, and I think my photographs are better for it. I know I am.

Music has also been important in my life. Through my research on the colonial period in America, I have come to love the music of William Billings (1746–1800). Billings was the first American-born composer and is primarily known for his church hymns. I have chosen selections of his hymn texts to accompany my photographs.

This book, and the companion exhibition *A Space for Faith*, are my tribute to New England's colonial meetinghouses and the people who built and used them. It is my hope that my photographs will illuminate both the graceful beauty and rich history embodied in these structures, and thereby awaken an interest in the importance of preserving this vital part of our national heritage.

Paul Wainwright

Atkinson, New Hampshire
January 2009

Photographs

Majestic God our muse inspire,
And fill us with seraphic fire.
Augment our swells, our tones refine,
Performance ours, the glory Thine.

Invocation

Rocky Hill Meeting House (1785), Amesbury, Massachusetts, 2004

Box Pews, Olde Meeting House (1755), Danville, New Hampshire, 2004

Sunlight on Pews, Old German Meeting House (1772), Waldoboro, Maine, 2007

Jaffrey Meeting House (1775), with Cloud, Jaffrey, New Hampshire, 2006

Door and Window, Old Meeting House (1773) (the interior was completed in 1774),
Sandown, New Hampshire, 2004

Alna Meetinghouse (1789), Alna, Maine, 2007

Door and Windows, Old Narragansett Church (1707), Wickford, Rhode Island, 2007

Pulpit Detail, Chestnut Hill Meeting House (1769), Millville, Massachusetts, 2006

Pew Bench, Rocky Hill Meeting House (1785), Amesbury, Massachusetts, 2007

Hour Glass, Old Meeting House (1773), Sandown, New Hampshire, 2007

Let tyrants shake their iron rod,
And slav'ry clank her galling chains.
We fear them not, we trust in God,
New England's God forever reigns.

Chester

Door, Olde Meeting House (1755), Danville, New Hampshire, 2004

Gate Detail, Chestnut Hill Meeting House (1769), Millville, Massachusetts, 2007

Old Trinity Church (1771), Brooklyn, Connecticut, 2007

Door and Windows, Rockingham Meetinghouse (1787), Rockingham, Vermont, 2007

Door and Windows, Old Meeting House (1745), Hampstead, New Hampshire, 2005

Box Pews, Chestnut Hill Meeting House (1769), Millville, Massachusetts, 2006

Pews and Window, Gosport Chapel (1800), Star Island, New Hampshire, 2006

Doors, Friends Meeting House (1706), Pembroke, Massachusetts, 2006

Looking Across Balcony, Rockingham Meetinghouse (1787), Rockingham, Vermont, 2007

First Parish Meeting House (1747), Cohasset, Massachusetts, 2006

Steeple, Old South Meeting House (1729), Boston, Massachusetts, 2008

Awake, my heart; arise, my tongue,
Prepare a tuneful voice;
In God, the life of all my joys
Aloud will I rejoice.

Andover

Old Meeting House (1773), Sandown, New Hampshire, 2006

Door Detail, Langdon Meeting House & Town Hall (1801), Langdon, New Hampshire, 2008

Brooklyn Meeting House (1771), at Dawn, Brooklyn, Connecticut, 2007

Box Pews and Windows, Olde Meeting House (1755), Danville, New Hampshire, 2007

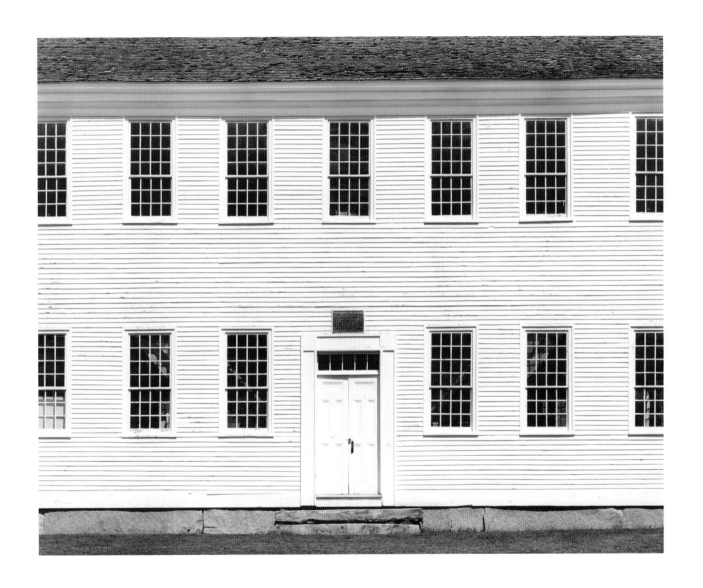

Webster Meetinghouse (1791), Webster, New Hampshire, 2005

Sun on Window Sill, Old Walpole Meetinghouse (1772), South Bristol, Maine, 2007

Window Detail, Old Meeting House (1773), Sandown, New Hampshire, 2004

Graffiti, Rocky Hill Meeting House (1785), Amesbury, Massachusetts, 2004

Door and Windows, Lempster Meetinghouse (1794). Lempster, New Hampshire, 2006

Door, West Parish Meetinghouse (1717), West Barnstable, Massachusetts, 2006

Door, Chestnut Hill Meeting House (1769), Millville, Massachusetts, 2006

Now shall my inward joys arise,
And burst into a song;
Almighty Love inspires my heart,
And Pleasure tunes my tongue.

Africa

Roof Beams, Old Ship Meetinghouse (1681), Hingham, Massachusetts, 2008

Upstairs, Old Trinity Church (1771), Brooklyn, Connecticut, 2007

Looking in Through Old Glass, Rocky Hill Meeting House (1785), Amesbury, Massachusetts, 2007

Freemont Meeting House (1800), Fremont, New Hampshire, 2006

Spindles, Old Meeting House (1773), Sandown, New Hampshire, 2007

Key, Olde Meeting House (1755), Danville, New Hampshire, 2007

Key Hole, Foster Town House (1796), Foster, Rhode Island, 2007

Key, Old German Meeting House (1772), Waldoboro, Maine, 2007

Key, Harrington Meeting House (1775), Pemaquid, Maine, 2007

Key, Old Meeting House (1773), Sandown, New Hampshire, 2007

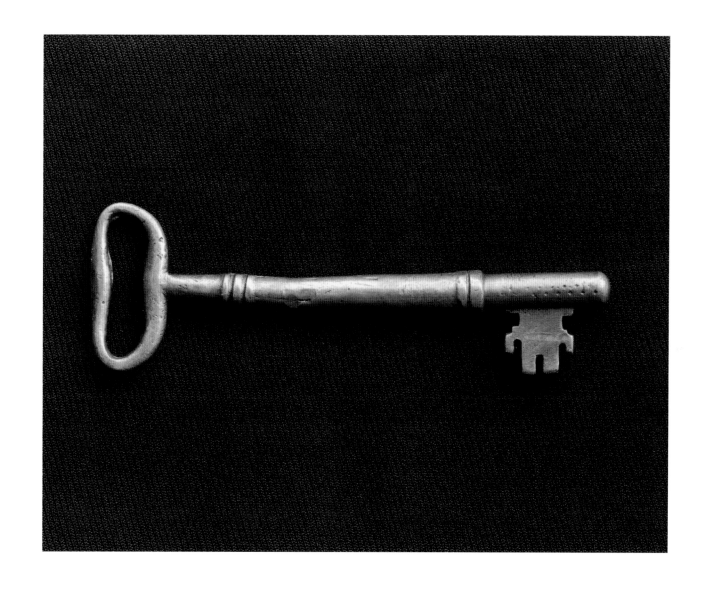

Key, Chestnut Hill Meeting House (1769), Millville, Massachusetts, 2007

Attic, Freemont Meeting House (1800), Fremont, New Hampshire, 2007

Old Glass (from Outside), Canaan Meeting House (1793), Canaan, New Hampshire, 2007

There is a land of pure delight,
Where saints immortal reign,
Infinite day excludes the night,
And pleasures banish pain.

Jordan

Windows, Beam, and Ceiling, Chestnut Hill Meeting House (1769), Millville, Massachusetts, 2007

Door and Windows, Canaan Meeting House (1793), Canaan, New Hampshire, 2006

Back of Old Walpole Meetinghouse (1772), South Bristol, Maine, 2007

Pulpit and Sounding Board, Olde Meeting House (1755), Danville, New Hampshire, 2007

Door Handle, Old Meeting House (1773), Sandown, New Hampshire, 2004

Box Pews, Freemont Meeting House (1800), Fremont, New Hampshire, 2004

Curved Beam, Olde Meeting House (1755), Danville, New Hampshire, 2004

Hook on Pew Door, Rocky Hill Meeting House (1785), Amesbury, Massachusetts, 2007

Looking Out Through Old Glass, Old Meeting House (1773), Sandown, New Hampshire, 2007

Sounding Board and Lamp, Old Walpole Meetinghouse (1772), South Bristol, Maine, 2007

When Jesus wept, the falling tear
In mercy flowed beyond all bound.
When Jesus groan'd, a trembling fear
Seiz'd all the guilty world around.

When Jesus Wept

Box Pews, Looking Down, Rocky Hill Meeting House (1785), Amesbury, Massachusetts, 2004

Pew Door #50, Rocky Hill Meeting House (1785), Amesbury, Massachusetts, 2007

Box Pews, Old Meeting House (1773), Sandown, New Hampshire, 2004

Window and Pew, Old Trinity Church (1771), Brooklyn, Connecticut, 2007

Trinity Church (1793), Cornish, New Hampshire, 2006

Stairs, Olde Meeting House (1755), Danville, New Hampshire, 2007

Window, Pews, and Lamp, Old Walpole Meetinghouse (1772), South Bristol, Maine, 2007

Pulpit Window, Alna Meetinghouse (1789), Alna, Maine, 2007

Back of Rocky Hill Meeting House (1785), Amesbury, Massachusetts, 2006

Window, Pews, and Ceiling, Old Narragansett Church (1707), Wickford, Rhode Island, 2007

Box Pews, Old Trinity Church (1797), Holderness, New Hampshire, 2006

With heav'nly weapons I have fought
The Battles of the Lord.
Finished my course, and kept the Faith
And wait the sure Reward.

Chesterfield

Old German Meeting House (1772), from Graveyard, Waldoboro, Maine, 2007

Olde Meeting House (1755), from Graveyard, Danville, New Hampshire, 2007

Harrington Meeting House (1775), from Graveyard, Pemaquid, Maine, 2007

Windows, Beams, and View of Graveyard, Olde Meeting House (1755), Danville, New Hampshire, 2007

Looking Out Through Old Glass, Chestnut Hill Meeting House (1769), Millville, Massachusetts, 2007

Harpswell Meeting House (1757), from Graveyard, Harpswell, Maine, 2007

Chestnut Hill Meeting House (1769), from Graveyard, Millville, Massachusetts, 2007

Gravestones and Window, Pelham Town Hall (1743), Pelham, Massachusetts, 2006

Window and View of Graveyard, Old Trinity Church (1797), Holderness, New Hampshire, 2006

Essay

The Birth of a Meetinghouse: Pelham, Massachusetts

In 1739 a land surveyor from Worcester, Massachusetts, was directed to go to an uninhabited area on a ridge on the east side of the Connecticut River Valley to lay out a tract of six equal ranges running east to west. Following the instructions given him by his employers, he was to set aside ten acres in the center for a meetinghouse, burying place, and training field to serve the Lisbourne Propriety as the center of its new community. According to town historian C. O. Parmenter, writing in 1898, the proprietors voted in 1740 for a meetinghouse "48 feet in length and 36 in width," and chose a committee of five men to superintend the raising of its frame. The committee, in turn, selected two local carpenters who had recently moved into the district to direct the work. Thomas and his brother John Dick had previous experience raising meetinghouses in neighboring Shutesbury and Petersham, and they were chosen to build the frame and complete the project.

In accordance with a contract that still survives in the vault in the Pelham Community Center, the brothers promised to raise a house similar to one they had erected for the town at Harvard, Massachusetts. In addition, the carpenters agreed to make a pew for the minister, a deacons' seat, and a pulpit and overhead canopy similar to the ones they had built in Harvard, to put together a gallery supported on four turned pillars, and to install "a body of seats for both men and women." They also agreed to paint the windows, doors, weather boards, troughs, and cornice with "askie color" (a Scottish term for ashy gray).

During the next two years, Thomas and John Dick set aside time to go through the house lots selecting and felling the best and straightest tall oaks, pines, and chestnuts, carting the timber to the ten-acre site, where they stacked and dried it. Because they knew the structure would not be heated, they marked off a spot where the main doorway and largest span of windows faced directly south, an alignment that placed the pulpit on the north side. They laid a foundation of stones. Then, after painstakingly squaring, trimming, and numbering each of about 200 timber pieces, they issued a notice to all men over the age of sixteen living in the propriety—now renamed the town of Pelham, Massachusetts—to meet them at sunrise of the next morning to assist in the raising. At least twenty families "of Good Conversation" helped them in this endeavor, many of them recent immigrants from northern Ireland, and mostly "of the Presbyterian Persuasion." They were also joined by neighbors from the first and second precincts of nearby Hadley, now the town of Amherst.

The day of raising was spent in concentrated communal labor. The first step was to install and secure the four ground sills. Then, having prepared six vertical "bents" or frame sections, teams of men using gin poles, heavy rigging, tackle, and winches raised each bent to a vertical position and slid the ends into the mortises in the sills. They were assisted by up to thirty men equipped with "pickpoles"—iron-tipped poles between fifteen and twenty feet long—to steady each piece until they had inserted the roof plates to make up the basic frame. Each piece was secured with tapered oak "treenails"—wooden pegs beaten in with a sledgehammer. At noontime the exhausted men sat on the sills to consume the provisions prepared by the women and children who attended them. In the afternoon, again using gins,

spars, and tackle, they inserted and locked in the six roof trusses, the principal rafters, and the ridgepole. At the end of the day, after they had secured and pinned the final piece of the frame, Thomas and John Dick and their key assistants climbed to the roof and led the assembled crowd singing a Presbyterian hymn to memorialize the occasion.

Over the next year, Thomas and John gradually finished the structure, enclosing it with boards, laying the under floor, boarding and shingling the roof, clapboarding the sides and ends, hanging doors, putting in hinges and window frames, installing casement windows, and building a gallery and stairwells. They followed traditional "New England" norms for locating the pulpit directly opposite the main door, installing a folding communion table at its base, and decorating and painting the canopy. At times they received new directions from the committee supervising their work. They were told to improve the pulpit, making it "for Dignity like unto Hadley third [precinct]"—now the town of Amherst, Massachusetts—a shift from the original instructions to make it similar to the one in Harvard. A special committee provided glass and finished the underpinning before the onset of winter. Another committee charged John Conkey with building a rail fence around the burying place, each rail ten feet long.

When completed, the new meetinghouse looked very much like an English barn—but with two important exceptions. First was the compass (or semicircular) pediment over the main door; agricultural structures in New England never used these ornaments. Second was the number and size of its twenty-six windows, each containing two sashes of 12 panes each—or a total of 624 panes. Barns were never glazed in early New England, because glass was an imported item. One window in particular, the pulpit window located midway between the first and second floors, stood out above the others. This window was surmounted by a half-circle top and provided light for the clergyman to read his sermon. It identified the structure as a meetinghouse. Within, galleries rose on the three sides facing the pulpit, the stairwells ascending to them placed in the corners. Benches and the single pew remained unpainted, but a coat of blue color was applied to the pulpit and "sounding board"—the overhead canopy designed to disperse the clergyman's voice.

On August 30, 1744, or about four years after the proprietors had voted to build the meetinghouse, the Reverend Robert Abercrombie was ordained at a ceremony presided over by the Reverend Jonathan Edwards of Northampton, who had recommended him to the Pelham congregation. The ceremony closed with singing of psalms and hymns taken from Isaac Watts' collection and led by deacons serving as choristers—the first of many hundreds of songs echoing within the meetinghouse space. That same year the first unmarked graves were being dug in the burying ground on its northern edge; and within a few years after that the first carved and decorated gravestones appeared. The first "necessaries" (outhouses) were dug and covered for the convenience of the assembled congregation; the first horse-sheds, horseblocks, and "Sabbathday-houses" (shelters heated by a large fireplace) were built for those who came from long distances; the first signposts and taverns were erected for occasional travelers who came that way. The community's collective history had begun.

Pelham's experience building and celebrating its new meetinghouse was representative of a widespread process in New England that characterized the creation of towns and their surrounding landscape for much of its early history. By rough count, approximately 2,000 houses of worship were raised in the two-hundred-year period between 1630 and 1830—about one for every one hundred fifty families.

The Role of the Meetinghouse in Early America

In keeping with Reformed Calvinist practices, a meetinghouse simultaneously served as a house of worship and as the town's secular meeting hall. As in Pelham between 1739 and 1744, the decision to locate, build, and maintain a meetinghouse was a municipal matter; all changes had to be approved at town or parish meetings. Except in Rhode Island, which lacked an instituted church, most New England colonial towns established churches of the Congregational or Presbyterian denominations as the publicly supported "orthodox" religions. Each new community had to be recognized by the colonial legislature. The town was obliged to hire a schoolteacher, build a schoolhouse, and keep title deeds and church records. It was also obliged to provide an established form of Christianity by hiring an "orthodox" and educated Protestant minister, giving him a house lot, or "glebe," and building a meetinghouse to hold weekly Sabbath exercises—all paid for by "rates," or property taxes.

When referring to these structures, colonial contracts and legal documents used the term *meetinghouse* instead of our more common term *church*. Most New Englanders in the seventeenth and eighteenth centuries were Protestant dissenters who had set aside the forms and liturgy of the Church of England. The Reverend Richard Mather, one of the leading divines of early Massachusetts history, told his Dorchester congregation that calling a structure a *church* was not sanctioned by the Bible. "There is no just ground in Scripture to apply such a trope as *church* to a place of assembly." Like all Puritans—indeed like all Reformed Protestants—he considered the term *church* as a body of covenanted Christians.

Because each church organization was a separate entity and made its own liturgical and architectural decisions, each was responsible for the form and dimensions of its meetinghouse.

Architectural Origins of New England Meetinghouses

In designing their meeting-houses, New England Puritans favored forms of architecture similar to those employed by Reformed congregations in Scotland, the Netherlands, and France in the sixteenth and early seventeenth centuries. Unlike Anglican churches and Catholic cathedrals, these structures were purposefully plain. Reformed believers designed their houses of worship to bring the congregations as close as possible to the word of God as interpreted by their clergymen. They banished things such as ritualized worship, crosses, statues, and stained-glass windows that distracted the congregation from focusing on the preaching of God's word. All reflected a common desire to improve acoustics through small theaters centered on the pulpit, created by using floor benches and one or more tiers of upper galleries or elevated pews. Typically these structures were topped by a centrally mounted turret and bell, whose ropes hung in the center of the main aisle.

When they came to the New World in the early seventeenth century, English Puritans faced both an opportunity and a dilemma. In England, Scotland, and the northern Netherlands, existing Christian church buildings were available in virtually every parish. During periods of Puritan ascendancy, and especially during the Commonwealth period, these structures were typically stripped and refitted as meetinghouses for Reformed services. In New England, obviously, colonists did not have older Anglican or Catholic churches that could be refitted, yet they had an immediate need for houses of worship to accommodate large numbers of immigrants. And they also had to provide for defense. At least a few early meetinghouses were little more than forts, some made of horizontal logs set into corner posts, surrounded by palisades, guardhouses, or elevated lookout turrets. These were raised as much against the settlers' French, Dutch, and Spanish enemies as against the surrounding Native Americans. Many early communities even assembled in animal barns, a practice that led to the popular practice of calling the meetinghouse the "Lord's Barn."

Once a community was more settled, however, builders again began to draw on the Reformed Protestant heritage for inspiration. While Reformed Dutch meetinghouses raised in Long Island and the New York colony assumed octagonal shapes in line with earlier practice in the Netherlands, seventeenth-century New England meetinghouses tended to be one of two kinds. First was a "long house," a stablelike building with a pitched roof where the pulpit was raised for better hearing. A second type was square or almost square, often built with one or two tiers of galleries to accommodate large congregations—a practice probably derived from sixteenth- and seventeenth-century Huguenots. These were typically covered by a high-pitched "four square" or hipped roof; a central turret, accessible from within, served as a lookout or a place to hang a bell. They ranged in dimensions from 20 by 20 feet or 24 by 24 feet to as large as 50 by 50 feet or even 75 by 51 feet (the Old Cedar in Boston). Like the old Huguenot temples, these houses of worship were pulpit-oriented and top-heavy in the sense that additional seats were provided by building pews attached to the roof beams or adding a second tier of galleries over the first.

More than three hundred of these early types of meetinghouses were built over the seventy-five years between 1640 and 1715, now termed the "first period" of meetinghouse building. Only one still stands, though it has been altered many times: the 1681 First Parish in Hingham, Massachusetts, a classic foursquare design that was expanded and modified in the mid-eighteenth century and again in the early twentieth century. In a final restoration in the 1930s, architects left the curved roof members exposed—the original feature whose contours produced the name "Old Ship."

Few reliable illustrations of first-period meetinghouses are available. The number of formal pews was minimal, the bulk of seating provided by benches. An interesting visual aspect of the outside of these meetinghouses was often the ornamental roof fixtures called "pyramids" or "pinnacles," mounted at the gables and on the turret.

Meetinghouses of the Second Period

Beginning in the early eighteenth century a new type of meetinghouse appeared in New England that reflected the gradual but substantive cultural and liturgical changes taking place in the region. Built between 1715 and 1800, these "second-period" meetinghouses retained most of the internal characteristics of the first-period meetinghouse while radically Georgianizing the exterior so that they came to resemble Anglican churches. Several things happened at once. For one thing, gable roofs rising about ten feet above the plate began replacing earlier, steeper hipped roofs, which rose about twenty feet above the plate. Votes taken by towns now alluded to "flat roofs," "straight roofs," "English roofs," and roofs built in "barn fashion." This change was accompanied by a characteristic lengthening of the structure. Typical footprints now were rectangular, 40 by 30 feet, 45 by 35 feet, or 50 by 40 feet. Sometimes outside stairwell porches were added—either a single one to the front or twin porches at the ends.

Equally important were changes to the architectural norms by which meetinghouses were publicly defined. For example, the pyramids or pinnacles of first-period structures either disappeared entirely or were converted into a single steeple topped with a spire. The first sign of this change came in a debate held at the September 1710 town meeting in Chelmsford, Massachusetts, over how to complete the turret of the new meetinghouse. After a number of meetings, a consensus was finally reached to concur with the committee's proposals to finish everything except the steeple. Although they finally decided against one, the simple act of considering a steeple held far-reaching religious implications because a steeple publicly designated the meetinghouse as a house of worship—not simply a gathering place for civic and religious life. This was a crucial turning point. It was not until four years later in 1714 that the first steeples in New England appeared in Boston—when the New North, the Brattle Square, and the New South congregations all built meetinghouses with an attached belltower and a spired steeple. Even so, most second-period meetinghouses lacked bell towers and bells. Towns instead continued to announce meeting times by beating a drum, sounding a trumpet, or simply raising a red flag or suspending it from a roof or turret. In some Connecticut Valley towns the shell of a West Indian conch (a large sea snail) was blown like a trumpet.

While steeples were rare, the meetinghouse raised in Brooklyn, Connecticut, offers a good example of how early meetinghouses and bell towers were financed and how competing religious sects sometimes rivaled one another for a share of the action. In 1769 the town of Brooklyn voted for a new meetinghouse to replace its old one. A prime advocate of this vote was Colonel Israel Putnam, a hero of the French and Indian wars and the object of much adulation. The largest taxpayer in town, however, was a new resident, Colonel Godfrey Malbone, a wealthy Anglican whose mansion in Newport, Rhode Island, had been burned by a mob protesting the Stamp Act. Malbone cultivated an extensive farm in Brooklyn with the assistance of black slaves. Facing an assessment of two hundred pounds, Malbone quickly organized like-minded individuals into an Anglican parish and built Trinity Church, completing it before his tax was due. Faced with a decline in revenues, the town in turn voted in 1771 that Putnam and his friends "may build a Steeple at one end of the new Meeting House that

is to be built…provided that they will build [it] at their own cost." They did so, apparently copying a Massachusetts model. Historian Edmund W. Sinnott, who reports these events in *Meetinghouse and Church in Early New England*, tells us there was a touch of romance (and irony) in the story when Israel Putnam's son Daniel married Malbone's daughter and became the senior warden of Trinity.

Another prominent feature of the second-period meetinghouse is the half-circle or compass-topped pulpit window—the type that had appeared in Pelham. Examples survive in many meetinghouses, including Alna, South Bristol, and Harpswell, Maine; Brooklyn, Connecticut; and Rocky Hill, in Amesbury, Massachusetts. This is the hallmark of the second-period New England meetinghouse. Like the standing bell tower and the steeple, it drew from a larger European tradition of ecclesiastic architecture where the compass-topped window was used by all denominations; it was a European signature, so to speak, transferred to the New World. But most New England meetinghouse builders used half-circle tops only on the pulpit window, leaving all other windows rectangular. It was a way of preserving their separation from the Anglican Church. By contrast, builders of Anglican houses of worship installed compass windows throughout the building, as they did in Wickford, Rhode Island, in 1707. At the same time, however, wealthy urban Congregational parishes broke this rule and used round-topped windows throughout their meetinghouses, among them those erected in Boston between 1699 and 1721 and mid-eighteenth-century meetinghouses in Ipswich, Massachusetts, and New Haven, Connecticut. Today, only the 1729 Old South meetinghouse in Boston is a surviving example of this practice.

Despite the fact that towns and parishes were governed by their own locally elected (and highly independent) committees, a noticeable similarity prevailed in second-period meetinghouses. This resemblance arose because framers and carpenters were constantly told to imitate each other's work in an effort to keep up with their neighboring communities. Just as Thomas and John Dick were instructed to copy the Harvard and Hadley "dignities" in Pelham, other communities replicated not only each other's pulpits and pulpit surrounds, but their overhead canopies or sounding boards, the wainscoting of their benches, their communion tables, pews, turrets, belfries, bell towers, and stairwell porches. They also copied each other's dimensions, stud heights, framing patterns, roofs, and seating plans. For example, the town of Rockingham, Vermont, passed three votes when they agreed to build a new meetinghouse in 1787. The first was "that the committee build the town House just as large as [the] Charlestown [New Hampshire] meeting house as to the square of it"; the second, "to build two porches one at each end"; and the third, "to have the plan of the inside of said house agreeable to the inside of the Meeting House in Charlestown." The result was a twin-porch struc-

ture that stands in that town to this day. In fact, twin-porch meetinghouses (such as those in Jaffrey and Temple) were so common in southern and central New Hampshire that these became a regional identifying feature. By the same token, single-porch meetinghouses became prevalent throughout Cape Cod, Maine, and coastal Massachusetts. Typical examples are the single-porch meetinghouses at Alna, Maine, and Amesbury, Massachusetts.

Towns even copied each other's colors. In 1760 Pomfret, Connecticut, painted its new meetinghouse orange (with white trim and chocolate doors); within a decade virtually every meetinghouse in Windham County adopted orange as its exterior color, making this something of a regional hallmark in eastern Connecticut. In New Hampshire, yellow and yellow-ochre prevailed. Surry, New Hampshire, copied the yellow hues of neighboring Keene, which had itself copied the yellows found in Jaffrey, Wilton, Temple, and Rindge. And colors often influenced informal naming practices. At least five meetinghouses were called "Old Yellar" (or some variant of this) from the original color of their clapboards long after these had faded to a dirty brown. New Haven's separatist meetinghouse was called "The Blue" after the color it acquired in 1765. "The Coffin" in Orford, New Hampshire, was known for its weather-blackened, unpainted exterior.

Over time, second-period meetinghouse builders began accentuating their embrace of the Georgian style. One method was increasingly to use wood to imitate stone construction, which usually involved an understanding of classical architectural "orders," or decorating modes. Even plain second-period meetinghouses were finished with Georgian-period motifs in this manner. Doorways and windows, for example, were adorned with Doric, Tuscan, and Corinthian orders, carpenters liberally applying molded and shaped wood sheathing to simulate stone much as painters simulated marble when decorating pulpits and pulpit surrounds. Ceilings were shaped into curved covings; the eaves of roofs acquired cornices and modillions. Pulpits were ornamented with dentils and fluted pillars. The classic triangular-pedimented front door found in Hampstead, New Hampshire, has the same stonelike presence as the more rural one found in Millville, Massachusetts, and even the one in Rockingham, Vermont. Equally stonelike are the flat pediments at the main doors of Danville and Lempster, New Hampshire, as well as the entry in Webster, New Hampshire.

This desire to suggest stone construction in wood may explain why many towns raising second-period meetinghouses after 1790 painted their meetinghouses with varieties of "stone" color. However, towns seldom if ever attempted to rusticate their exterior clapboards with wood panels scored to simulate laid stone, a technique found in some domestic dwelling houses of similar date in New England. Most meetinghouses were covered with pine clapboards, though a few, such as in Alna and South Bristol, Maine, used shingles for at least part of their exterior covering.

Inside, second-period meetinghouse builders retained the traditional Reformed layout by keeping the elevated pulpit close to the surrounding benches, pews, and galleries, and preserving both the acoustical benefits of the overhead canopy and the convenience of the folding communion table. They also retained the perpendicular quality of the structure, with interior space as vertical as it was horizontal. While only one "triple decker" meetinghouse is now still standing (the Old South meetinghouse in Boston), there may have been as many as fifty in use by 1770. A hint of this verticality is found in the Millville and Danville meetinghouses, whose smaller dimensions reinforce the cramped closeness of the pulpit to the galleries and pews.

Still, the use of Georgian-style architectural details permeates the interior of these second-period meetinghouses. Examples include the heavily built-up front of the pulpit in Millville, Massachusetts, and the octagonal canopy, or "sounding board," in Danville, New Hampshire—seemingly supported by fluted pilasters but actually attached to the walls and ceiling by heavy iron rods. Elsewhere, turned spindles decorated the balustrade apertures in individual pews such as the ones in Millville, Massachusetts. Again, the interior colors tended to reflect the effort to use wood to simulate stone. Some towns even went so far as to marbleize these surfaces. Sandown and Rocky Hill marbleized their pillars and pulpit surrounds with blue and white; Ipswich, New Hampshire, painted its pulpit poppy red, grained to imitate red marble.

Denominational Differences

Second-period Reformed meetinghouses maintained denominational differences from those structures raised by Anglicans. Internally there was no ritualistic main alley leading from the door to the pulpit in a Congregational or Presbyterian meetinghouse as there was in an Anglican church; there was no altar, chancel, or permanent communion table. Where Anglicans looked out of compass-headed windows and knelt on cushions as they did in Brooklyn, Connecticut, Presbyterians and Congregationalists looked out of square windows, sat in benches or chairs, and stood up to sing. Bells were part of the Anglican ceremony, but bells simply told time in a Congregational or Presbyterian meetinghouse, and typically when a bell tower existed it did not provide the principal access to the meetinghouse. Some exterior embellishments to the meetinghouse were strictly limited to Anglican houses of worship. The only two broken-scroll pediments known to have been installed on New England meetinghouses were on St. Paul's Church in Wickford, Rhode Island, and Christ Church in Stratford, Connecticut. Quakers,

on the other hand, adhered to the traditional simplicity of their sect. The two doors of the Quaker meetinghouse in Pembroke, Massachusetts, reveal one for males, another for females—reflecting a traditional Protestant seating plan that was retained by Quakers well into the nineteenth century.

On another level, however, provincial America generated its own wood-frame building style in the eighteenth century that often disregarded denominational differences in ecclesiastic structures or, as historian Carl Lounsbury suggests, expressed a shared Protestant attitude toward church architecture. Depending on their location, meetinghouses raised by Congregationalists, Presbyterians, Anglicans, Quakers, and Baptists assumed a regional and "North American" identity. In 1793, when an Anglican congregation raised a meetinghouse in Cornish, New Hampshire, they hired Philip Tabor to do the work; he had recently built the Congregational meetinghouse in nearby Washington, New Hampshire. While both structures conformed to the criteria of each sect, their buildings probably had more similarities than differences. Take the matter of sash-hung windows. The same variety of 25-over-20 panes at the Anglican church in Cornish, New Hampshire, is not much different from the 20-over-20 panes at Rockingham, Vermont. Much the same can be said of the first Lutheran meetinghouse in New England in Waldoboro, Maine, which differs from the meetinghouses of its Congregational neighbors only in the placing of the front stairwell porch on the gable end.

The Meetinghouse as the Center of Secular and Religious Life

As symbols of community authority, meetinghouses served a variety of secular and public uses both inside the structure and immediately outside it. Generally these activities were dominated by adult men. Annual town meetings—attended principally by men—were routinely convened in meetinghouses, though adjournments might be reconvened in the hall of the nearest tavern. Capital trials were routinely conducted in meetinghouses. They served as temporary barracks for soldiers on the march and as places to negotiate treaties with Native Americans. Their grounds served as a place of

punishment, providing a setting for wooden stocks and "cages" (portable jails), as well as a site for executions and execution sermons. A townsman who had succeeded in killing a wolf would display its head on the meetinghouse door to earn the four-pence bounty. There was no heat in these structures (because a fire in such a large building would be impossible to extinguish), and gunpowder was routinely stored there by the local militia. "Banns" (proposed marriage announcements) were posted on them. These activities continued well into the eighteenth century. Public protests, culminating in the

Boston Tea Party, were held in the Old South meetinghouse in Boston in the 1770s. And, in response, during the British occupation of Boston in 1775, meetinghouses were burnt for firewood or converted into horse-riding rings by British occupiers.

At the same time, however, the weekly use of the meetinghouse for religious exercises identified it primarily as a sacred place. What was it like to observe the Sabbath in a New England meetinghouse? Basically, it was like going to school—only it was a school for everyone, not simply for children. The interior of the meetinghouse itself was arranged in rows with a desk and deacons' pews supervising the congregation. Small folding desks were often provided to parishioners for taking notes. And most of the town showed up at these exercises because attendance was mandatory. By law, residents of Connecticut and Massachusetts were obliged to listen to two written sermons each week—one in the Sabbath morning and a second in the afternoon; both were timed by an hourglass and usually lasted for one or two hours. These sermons were accompanied by singing, prayers, and invocations, by witnessing public confessions, and by listening to the clergyman or a deacon read the Bible.

Seating places and exiting procedures were assigned by a committee chosen for that purpose. Most Reformed denominations in the seventeenth century required each sex to sit separately, the men to the left of the pulpit, the women to the right. The best places were benches nearest the pulpit, as well as the wall pews to either side. In making their determinations, seating committees were told to give precedence to age, importance, and estate. The entire community was thus ranked by the places to which they were assigned, no one being allowed to move up until the death of someone ahead of them. Widows and unmarried women sat in one section; unpropertied men in another; apprentices, servants, and slaves in another, often upstairs in the gallery. Small children usually sat near the "soldiers' seats" at the entrance.

Making sure that these rules were followed were "tithingmen," vigilant adults armed with a stick or a truncheon with a brass tip on one end. This was an office codified into law after 1721 but practiced many decades earlier. Called "grotesque" by one nineteenth-century historian, tithingmen have left a legacy of colonial humor. According to the "diary" of the fictitious English traveler Obadiah Turner, a tithingman who had been assigned the duties of waking up sleepers at the Lynn, Massachusetts, meetinghouse, armed his stick with a foxtail at one end and a thorn on the other. Strutting around the meetinghouse, he spied a man sleeping in the corner and gave him a "grevious prick" on his finger. The sleeper, dreaming he had been attacked by a large rodent, sprang up and shouted "cussed be the woodchuck." The diarist concluded that the man was "much abashed...[and] would not again go to sleep in the meeting."

Gradual alterations to the rule of seating by sexes led to the first significant change to Protestant worship services in eighteenth-century New England. After 1700, people of wealth and prominence were allowed to build pews for themselves and their families. Initially these were kept separate, male pews for men and female pews for women. But eventually families were seated together—"promiscuously," as the records termed it. However, many upland and rural parishes largely kept to the old ways because people did not have the resources to build pews.

Another shift was the reintroduction of passive forms of Anglican liturgy that had been banished by sixteenth- and seventeenth-century Puritans. The Brattle Street congregation, formed in Boston by a newly wealthy group of merchants, reintroduced the Lord's Prayer into the service when they founded their church in 1699. Other Boston congregations reintroduced the reading of Scripture during the divine service (a form of liturgy discouraged by the first generation of immigrants because it was seen as simply a rote exercise). This practice, too, evolved over time, and after 1730 congregations began to approve the reading of Scripture, usually when a patron was found who would provide the Bible and a case to put it in. By 1780 most congregations read Scripture. More important still were measures to increase church membership and give greater access to the two Puritan sacraments of baptism and communion. Many congregations gave up on the Puritan idea of publicly confessing one's religious experience before being allowed to baptize children and to take communion. The controversial "half-way" covenant allowed baptism to nonmembers; open membership to anyone not visibly corrupt (an Anglican practice) gave even greater access to communion.

An important element in the Sabbath exercise was singing the psalms. While the English Puritans who landed in the New World were trained in music, they were more interested in the literal accuracy of their translations. In 1636 they asked thirty scholars qualified in Hebrew to write a new version of the psalms under the editorship of the Reverend Richard Mather of Dorchester, Massachusetts, and the Reverends Thomas Welde and John Eliot of nearby Roxbury. Published in 1640, *The Whole Book of Psalms* was adopted by virtually all Massachusetts congregations and became known as the "Bay Psalm Book." Difficult to sing, the text also made it hard to pass musical knowledge to the next generation because musical instruments were not used in the Puritan service. Eventually both the lack of psalmodies and the failure to understand musical notation led to a breakdown in singing practices. Critics saw the manner of singing the psalm as "rough, horrid verse" which "grated through the ear." Others saw it as a "drawling, quavering discord." The solution was to read the psalm each time it was sung. A leader, usually a deacon, read out a line of the psalm, and the congregation followed by singing that line. The deacon then read the second line of the psalm, and the congregational followed—and so on until the entire psalm was completed. Some psalms may have taken ten or twenty minutes to sing. This process was called "deaconizing the psalms" or "lining out," and more than anything else it reflected or characterized the Reformed service in a provincial setting where musical training was not available.

Alterations to this practice led to a second critical change in the Sabbath experience when measures were taken by the congregation to improve singing. Beginning in 1699, the same Brattle Street congregation that had introduced the Lord's Prayer into its service announced it would no longer line out its psalms but would sing them all the way through. They soon organized a school for singing "by rule," meaning they asked the congregants to begin on a suitable pitch and follow notes "prickt" on a page. Many congregations resisted this, thinking the practice was "Popish," but over the next 125 years they gradually fell into line, abandoning the old recitative manner one by one and replacing it with trained singers. Sometimes this was done piecemeal. A congregation might vote to sing all the way through in the morning service, but line out in the afternoon—

or the other way around. Other congregations deaconized the psalms only on communion days. Trained singers were given special pews on the floor and later moved into the first row of the gallery. Like seating families together, voting not to read the psalm represented a major shift in liturgical practice that brought them closer to the old Anglican tradition.

At this point, however, singing teachers skilled in musical composition began their extraordinary rise to fame by reviving psalms, hymns, and anthems sung "in the New England way." Led by composers such as William Billings, Daniel Read, and Ishmael Spicer, they generated an innovative form of music that combined the best of the old singing tradition with a new American-inspired lyrical emphasis that has since characterized New England's religious music. Few of these men were professional musicians. Billings, in particular, who worked full time as a tanner in Boston, published his first collection in 1770. *The New England Psalm Singer: or, American Chorister* was the first American psalmody. He followed with six other collections, published between 1772 and his death in 1800. In eulogizing Billings, the Reverend William Bentley of Salem, Massachusetts, called "this self-taught man…the father of our New England music."

Strains on the Parish System

As New England's population continued to expand, the parish system under which established Congregational and Presbyterian churches were gathered also approached a point of breakdown. Fulfilling the requirements of founding an established church was never easy. There were constant problems associated with locating the proper site for the meetinghouse, determining its dimensions, and approving its form, pattern, and interior finish. Since attendance was mandatory, factions soon grew up that worked to have the meetinghouse placed nearest to them. If the town straddled a river, siting the structure on one side might create a dangerous crossing in the winter months for those on the other. This sometimes led to the resiting of the house itself. Twenty-two years after the Old German meetinghouse in Waldoboro, Maine, was built in 1772, the population had so shifted in that town that the house was pulled across the ice of the frozen Medomak River to its present location. The 1762 meetinghouse in Westmoreland, New Hampshire, became so inaccessible it was raised up

on logs and moved twice by oxen, each time from one hill to another: first in 1779 when it was moved to a new location two miles away; second in 1827 when it was moved another hundred feet. The first time it became stalled in the valley, and the men were about to abandon it. The promise of another barrel of rum, a common commodity during meetinghouse construction, inspired completion of the task.

Another cause of contention was the gradual appearance of alternate Protestant sects that did not have the advantage of legal recognition enjoyed by the Congregationalists and Presbyterians. This had been a problem for Anglican churches founded in Boston in the 1680s—which in the third and fourth decades of the eighteenth century greatly prospered there—and in other coastal communities, especially those in Connecticut. This caused great bitterness. One solution was to allow approved Protestant denominations (principally Anglicans, Baptists, and Quakers) who had paid for and regularly attended their own services to appeal and gain remission from

Congregational taxes—as happened after 1720 in both Connecticut and Massachusetts.

Perhaps the greatest strain on the parish system was the growing cost of the established church, especially the expense of ministers' salaries. This was a particularly heavy burden on towns in the newly settled uplands of Connecticut and Massachusetts and along the frontiers of New Hampshire and Maine. Inflation during the later years of the War for Independence and the financial problems of the post-war period exacerbated the problem. In some towns the Congregational churches never recovered their privileged position. They were faced with the rise of competing denominations and a series of short-tenured ministers, many of whom were unable to support themselves on their salaries, and were not always paid in full

The Demise of the Second-Period Meetinghouse

The gradual breakdown of the old parish system eventually led to two developments, one architectural and the other legal. First, it precipitated a new Federal type of meetinghouse, one built "according to the fashions of the present day" (as the town of Hinsdale, Massachusetts, termed it in 1797) and not in the Reformed style. The reasons were closely tied to the success of the American Revolution and the gradual withdrawal of town sponsorship of religious affairs. The initial prototypes were raised

under the supervision of architects such as Charles Bulfinch in 1789, but they came into full fruition with the publication of architectural planbooks compiled by Asher Benjamin after 1795. These new structures were Federal-period "churches" complete with a portico, an architecturally designed steeple, and a reorientation of the exterior so that the narrow end of the building faced the street. Interiors were rearranged to provide a long main aisle running from the portico to the pulpit; slip pews were introduced instead of box pews. These churchlike edifices were still technically meetinghouses in that they were raised as municipally owned structures using town money—though also with increasingly large amounts of privately pledged money. Their use became more and more restricted to sacred purposes.

The second development was more drastic and challenged the basis on which New England towns had gathered churches since the early seventeenth century: the disestablishment of religion in the four New England states where it was still practiced. The "standing order," as it was popularly known, was dissolved by state legislatures in 1807 in Vermont, 1817 in Connecticut, 1819 in New Hampshire, and 1832 in Massachusetts. This put the region in line with the new Federal constitution, whose first amendment banned the United States Congress from passing any laws respecting religion.

With the passage of these laws, each New England town was required to separate ownership of the meetinghouse into its two principal constituencies. Some towns, like Pelham, Massachusetts, assumed ownership of the meetinghouse when the congregation built and occupied its own church on a lot right next door to the meetinghouse in 1839. The town eventually converted its meetinghouse into a town house, and the building soon became known as the "Pelham Town Hall." Much the same thing happened in Washington, New Hampshire, whose Congregational society raised a new Gothic Revival house of worship in 1840 about a hundred feet from the

meetinghouse. Here, too, the town assumed ownership and maintenance of the meetinghouse, converting the gallery into a dance hall and the downstairs into a town house. In some instances, frugal New Englanders shared occupancy, separating the floors and placing the church upstairs and the town hall downstairs. This was done in Rindge and Hancock, New Hampshire, and in Lynnfield, Massachusetts. On the whole, however, especially in communities in Massachusetts and Connecticut, meetinghouses were almost always taken over by the churches that had previously used them. Examples include those in Cohasset, Hingham, Dedham, Groton, and Townsend in Massachusetts, and those in Farmington, Brooklyn, and Wethersfield, Connecticut.

In the end, the New England meetinghouse was an impermanent form. Of the estimated 1,000 second-period meetinghouses of the type illustrated in this volume, approximately 180 still stand, the majority of them hidden under renovations and additions. Of these, about 130 still serve as houses of worship for Congregational, Unitarian, or Baptist religious societies; 24 function as museums; and 15 are now town houses. What became of the others? After 1800 most urban churches pulled down their wood-frame meetinghouses and replaced them with expensive structures of stone or brick; rural congregations, or those who could not afford to rebuild, literally raised their meetinghouses a few feet off the ground and turned them ninety degrees so that the short side faced the street and then set them back down. The addition of a portico or entry porch completed their conversion into "churches." As for the rest, they were frequently sold and converted into barns or granges, or just demolished immediately and burned for firewood. A few served out their time as movie houses, rooming houses, or factories. These seldom survived. The 1748 meetinghouse in Hatfield, Massachusetts, was moved two miles north to a farm in the 1850s to serve as a storage shed and later as a tobacco-drying barn when it was given a new slate roof. In the 1970s, when the farmer who owned the property wanted to raze it, an attempt was made to save the structure by moving it across a highway. But the weight of the roof was so great that the structure collapsed in a wind storm during transit.

Fortunately, a few acts of serendipity, frugality, and good fortune saved a number of these meetinghouses for future generations. The survival of the Rocky Hill meetinghouse in Amesbury, Massachusetts, and the meetinghouses in Sandown and Danville, New Hampshire—all now operated as museums—are among the few untouched examples of the period. All three structures were in the care of their respective churches in the nineteenth and early twentieth centuries, with declining congregations. And all three were abandoned by their owners just as interest in preservation began in earnest in the region at the turn of the twentieth century. Rocky Hill

was taken over in 1941 by the Society for the Preservation of New England Antiquities (now Historic New England); Sandown in 1929 by the Old Meeting House Historical Association; and Danville in 1911 by the Olde Meeting House Association, a local preservation society. Similar stories apply to the meetinghouse in Rockingham, Vermont, now maintained by the town, and to the Lutheran meetinghouse in Waldoboro, Maine, which is now maintained by the German Protestant Society.

In many towns such as Lempster, New Hampshire, and Pelham, Massachusetts, it is fortunate that changes in demographics took place at just the right time to effect the preservation of the meetinghouse. After assuming sole ownership, Lempster leased its meetinghouse to the Silver Mountain Grange; the grange maintained it through the 1980s and then passed it on to a local preservation society. The meetinghouse in Pelham survived relatively intact because the town's population decreased in size in the nineteenth century, and what remained of it shifted toward the eastern boundary of Amherst, accessible by a branch of the local street railway. The few townspeople in the western portion of the town continued to use the building as their town hall. The town of Pelham still convenes there once a year and maintains its claim to have the oldest meetinghouse continually used for town meetings in America.

Conclusion

The superb photographs that fill this volume honor a small part of what remains of New England's colonial meetinghouses. The images are as disciplined as they are stunning. Each captures the intellectual and spiritual world of the early New England town meeting and its accompanying Protestant worshippers, and each does so without once attempting to depict the individuals themselves. Most of the photographs portray meetinghouses of the second period, a time when many of the earlier "Puritan" liturgical practices in the region were being replaced by quieter, more inclusive, more formal "Congregationalist" ones, and town houses and large public halls were gradually replacing meetinghouses

as the sites of town meetings that handled municipal business. Puritanism, in other words, had evolved into something less austere and more ritualized by the time most of these meetinghouses were raised.

The photographs in this volume are a fitting tribute to the architectural beauty of these surviving meetinghouses.

Peter Benes

Concord, Massachusetts
January 2009

Peter Benes is Cofounder and Director of the Dublin Seminar for New England Folklife.

Acknowledgments

I wish to thank the owners of the meetinghouses featured in this publication and in the corresponding museum exhibition for giving me access to their buildings, and for supplying information about their structures for the book, exhibition, and project web site, www.colonialmeetinghouses.com. I especially thank the "Custodians of the Keys," to use a term current at the time these places were built. Their love of these structures and their dedication to preserving them has made my efforts most enjoyable.

Many people have helped with preparing the manuscript for this publication. I would like to extend my thanks to Jane Montague Benes, Professor Kevin M. Sweeney, Lin Faye, Bonnie Bryant Hiller, Joseph Larson, Robert Lord Keyes, Sue Martin, and the Reverend John E. Denson, Jr. for their careful reading and thoughtful comments on the text. Thanks also to Jay Goldsmith, Vickie Wright, and Peter Randall for their help with editing and sequencing the photographs, and to Stephen Patterson, Andrew Epstein, Gary Chassman, Tillman Crane, Peter Baldwin, and Mary Virginia Swanson for their support.

I also extend my thanks to Peter Hoving and John Osborne for the delightful experience of working with them to produce the video essay entitled *Colonial Meetinghouses*, which tells the story of New England's colonial meetinghouses and my work to photograph them. This video essay can be viewed on the www.colonialmeetinghouses.com web site.

Selected Bibliography

Ayer, Mary Farwell. *The South Meeting-House, Boston, 1669–1729.* Boston: Clapp, 1905.

Benes, Peter. "Sky Colors and Scattered Clouds: The Decorative and Architectural Painting of New England Meeting Houses, 1738–1834." *New England Meeting House and Church: 1630–1850: 1979 Proceedings of the Dublin Seminar for New England Folklife.* Boston: Boston University Scholarly Publications, 1979.

Benes, Peter. "The Templeton 'Run' and the Pomfret 'Cluster': Patterns of Diffusion in Rural New England Meetinghouse Architecture, 1647–1822." *Old-Time New England* 68 (winter–spring 1978): 1–21.

Benes, Peter. "Twin-Porch versus Single-Porch Stairwells: Two Examples of Cluster Diffusion in Rural Meetinghouse Architecture." *Old-Time New England* 69 (1979): 44–68.

Benes, Peter, and Philip D. Zimmerman. *New England Meeting House and Church: 1630–1850: A Loan Exhibition Held at the Currier Gallery of Art, Manchester, New Hampshire.* Boston: Boston University Scholarly Publications, 1979.

Buggeln, Gretchen T. *Temples of Grace: The Material Transformation of Connecticut's Churches, 1790–1840.* Hanover, N.H.: University Press of New England, 2003.

Donnelly, Marian C. "New England Meetinghouses of the Seventeenth Century." *Old-Time New England* 47 (April–June 1957): 85-99.

Earle, Alice Morse. *The Sabbath in Puritan New England.* New York: Charles Scribner's Sons, 1891.

Garvan, Anthony N. B. *Architecture and Town Planning in Colonial Connecticut.* New Haven: Yale University Press, 1951.

Kelly, J. Frederick. *Early Connecticut Meeting Houses.* 2 vols. New York: Columbia University Press, 1948.

Jager, Ronald, and Sally Krone. *"… A Sacred Deposit": The Meetinghouse in Washington, New Hampshire.* Washington, N.H.: Randall, 1989.

Lounsbury, Carl. "God is in the Details: The Transformation of Ecclesiastical Architecture in Early-Nineteenth-Century America." *Vernacular Architecture Journal* 13, no. 1 (2006): 1–21.

Place, Charles A. "From Meeting House to Church New England." *Old-Time New England* 13 and 14 (October 1922 to July 1923).

Sinnott, Edmund W. *Meeting House and Church in Early New England.* New York: Bonanza Books, 1963.

Speare, Eva A. *Colonial Meeting-Houses of New Hampshire.* Littleton, N.H. Reginald M. Colby, Agent, 1938, Revised 1955.

Sweeney, Kevin M. "Meetinghouses, Town Houses, and Churches: Changing Perceptions of Sacred and Secular Space in Southern New England, 1720–1850." *Winterthur Portfolio* 28, no. 1 (spring 1993).

Wight, Charles A. *Some Old Time Meetinghouses of the Connecticut Valley.* Chicopee Falls, Mass.: Wight, 1911.

Winslow, Ola E. *Meetinghouse Hill, 1630–1783.* New York: Norton, 1972.

Index of Meetinghouses*

* This book uses the currently accepted *meetinghouse* (one word) except in captions and in this index, where the form employed by the property owner is used.

New Hampshire

Canaan	Canaan Meeting House (1793)	51, 55
Cornish	Trinity Church (1793)	69
Danville	Olde Meeting House (1755)	5, 15, 30, 44, 57, 60, 70, 78, 80
Fremont	Fremont Meeting House (1800)	42, 50, 59
Hampstead	Old Meeting House (1745)	19
Holderness	Old Trinity Church (1797)	75, 85
Jaffrey	Jaffrey Meeting House (1775)	7
Langdon	Langdon Meeting House & Town Hall (1801)	28
Lempster	Lempster Meetinghouse (1794)	35
Sandown	Old Meeting House (1773)	3, 8, 13, 27, 33, 43, 48, 53, 58, 62, 67
Star Island	Gosport Chapel (1800)	21
Webster	Webster Meetinghouse (1791)	31

Rhode Island

Foster	Foster Town House (1796)	45
Wickford	Old Narragansett Church (1707)	10, 74

Vermont

Rockingham	Rockingham Meetinghouse (1787)	18, 23

Additional Information

Project Web Site

Additional information about New England's colonial meetinghouses, including structures that were not included in this book, can be found on the project web site: www.colonialmeetinghouses.com. There you will find a wealth of information about each meetinghouse, including historical narratives, visitor information, and more photographs.

Traveling Exhibition

A traveling exhibition featuring a selection of photographs from the Colonial Meetinghouse Project is available to galleries, museums, and universities, and can be tailored to meet the needs of specific venues. In conjunction with the exhibition, the photographer is available to speak about his work, and can assist in arranging other programs such as presentations by prominent scholars. More information about the exhibition can be found on the project web site: www.colonialmeetinghouses.com.

Limited Edition Fine-Art Photographs

The original photographs featured in this book were made from four-by-five-inch, black-and-white sheet film, and were hand-printed in a traditional darkroom and later scanned by the artist for reproduction. All images from this project are available as museum-quality, limited edition fine-art photographic prints, and are offered in several sizes. Each photograph is hand-printed, selenium toned, and spotted by the photographer to archival standards; each print is signed and numbered. For information about purchasing original artwork, please contact the photographer directly, or visit: www.paulwainwrightphotography.com.